Lunch
boxes

Lunch boxes

Jennifer Joyce

To my stalwart lunch-box testers, Liam and Riley

MICHAEL JOSEPH

Published by the Penguin Group
Penguin Books Ltd, 80 Strand, London WC2R 0RL, England
Penguin Group (USA) Inc., 375 Hudson Street, New York, New York 10014, USA
Penguin Group (Canada), 90 Eglinton Avenue East, Suite 700, Toronto, Ontario, Canada M4P 2Y3
     (a division of Pearson Penguin Canada Inc.)
Penguin Ireland, 25 St Stephen's Green, Dublin 2, Ireland (a division of Penguin Books Ltd)
Penguin Group (Australia), 250 Camberwell Road,
     Camberwell, Victoria 3124, Australia (a division of Pearson Australia Group Pty Ltd)
Penguin Books India Pvt Ltd, 11 Community Centre,
     Panchsheel Park, New Delhi – 110 017, India
Penguin Group (NZ), cnr Airborne and Rosedale Roads, Albany,
     Auckland 1310, New Zealand (a division of Pearson New Zealand Ltd)
Penguin Books (South Africa) (Pty) Ltd, 24 Sturdee Avenue,
     Rosebank, Johannesburg 2196, South Africa

Penguin Books Ltd, Registered Offices: 80 Strand, London WC2R 0RL, England

www.penguin.com

First published 2005
1

Copyright © Jennifer Joyce, 2005

Illustrations © Katherina Manolessou

Design by Shiny Design

The moral right of the author has been asserted

Printed in Italy by Printer Trento S.r.l.

A CIP catalogue record for this book is available from the British Library

ISBN-13: 978–0–718–14874–4
ISBN-10: 0–718–14874–6

About the author

Living in the UK since 1991, Jennifer grew up in the US, eating a lot of peanut butter and jelly sandwiches in her lunch box. When she's not making packed lunches for her two sons, Liam and Riley, she can usually be found talking or writing about food. Currently, she writes monthly for *New Woman* and contributes to the *Weekend Telegraph*, *BBC Good Food* and *Olive* magazines. Books for Cooks and Divertimenti in London both host her weekly cookery courses. She is the sole author of two books: *Small Bites* (Dorling Kindersley) and *The Well-Dressed Salad* (Pavilion); and the co-author of *Diva Cooking* (Mitchell Beazley). Along with numerous appearances on the BBC's *Good Food Live*, she has presented two series for Taste CFN. Jennifer lives with her family in St Margarets.

Contents

About the author 5

Introduction 8

Health bits 10

A week's lunch plan and shopping list 15

Sandwiches, wraps and rolls 19

Snacks and dips 55

Salads 71

Stuff to make ahead 93

Sweets and treats 107

Index 122

Acknowledgements 124

Introduction

When my children started school, I set out with the best of intentions to make healthy and inventive lunches. But, like most people, the ham sandwich/crisps combo began to feature more often than not. Eventually, it became pure drudgery (for both them and me) and they moved on to school dinners. After a year of dreary menus, I decided to give lunch boxes another try – but this time with a serious make-over. It actually wasn't difficult; it just took a little creativity. During our experimentation there were big successes, lots of laughs, serious flops and even a few tears. Luckily, kids are truthful so I got a quick verdict about what was brilliant and what was chucked in the bin.

I asked every mother I know about their children's lunch-box menus and the differences were astounding. It ranged from 'only ham sandwiches' to 'adores sushi'. Children's taste buds are bewildering. One day they like something and the next week they don't. It's easy to get frustrated and give up, but patience, tenacity and strategic skills are highly recommended. Food they haven't eyeballed or tasted before is a sworn foreign enemy. Sometimes it takes three or four times to introduce new things and make them less frightening.

THE IMPORTANT THING IS TO TRY, AND KEEP TRYING.
The key to successful healthy lunch boxes is to build
them around something they like. Children have what I
call the 'CSS palate'. They like things that are creamy,
salty or sweet. I don't mean feed them fat, salt and
sugar, but choose ingredients with these characteristics –
creamy cheeses, soy sauce or sweet fruit. Find their
favourites and build on them. Crisps, biscuits and sweets
are all part of being a kid, so try to find a balance
between healthy snacks and a few treats as well. If a
little caramel sauce gets them to eat an apple a day,
celebrate it.

Once you've experimented a bit, make a list of your
kids' favourites and pin them up in the kitchen. This will
remind you what to shop for each week and encourage
diversity. Even if you only get one new thing from this
book, then at least that's something. A neighbourhood
friend, whose daughter was strictly 'ham and cheese',
was ecstatic to find that she now liked salami. It was
an epiphany for another mother to discover deli whole-
roasted chicken for sandwiches and salads. Whatever
you do, get inspired, and make lunch boxes more fun
for everyone.

Health bits

What does 'five a day' mean? A daily requirement means five handfuls of fruit and veg. Handful size is relative to the person – so one child's portion isn't that big. Eight grapes or a few cherry tomatoes would fit.

Try to vary the colours: orange, yellow and red means beta-carotene for eyes and Vitamin C for immunity. Green indicates calcium for bones and teeth. The darker and more intense the colour the better!

This is a list of some of the fruit and vegetables that you might be likely to put into lunch boxes in sandwiches, salads, dips or snacks. Most of them are considered 'superfoods', which are vegetables and fruit that contain an extraordinarily high level of vitamins, minerals, fibre, immunity boosters and antioxidants. Although this is not a full nutritional guide, it is a simple reminder of the important benefits these provide and why you should try to fit them in.

Fruit

Use with muffins, fruit salads and snacks, or with cottage or ricotta cheese. Try to leave the skins on fruit whenever possible for even more fibre.

Blackberries – an excellent source of Vitamin C, which is especially good for immunity and skin. They contain other nutrients for bones and eyesight.

Blueberries – rank at the top of all fruit or vegetables for highest antioxidants. A virtual powerhouse covering eyesight, skin, digestion, kidneys, bones, blood circulation, heart, anti-cancer and immunity.

Raspberries – very big on calcium, helping bones, teeth, digestion, hormones, skin, hair and nervous system, plus boosting immunity.

Strawberries – contain Vitamin K, which allows calcium to be absorbed. Also benefit immunity, bones, heart, nervous system, digestive system, kidneys, bladder and blood circulation.

Bananas – good slow-releasing energy food and advantageous for hormones, blood, digestion and heart.

Mangos – great source of beta-carotene for eyes, also good for immunity, digestion and bones.

Pineapples – rich in enzymes for reducing inflammation. Also good for heart, anti-cancer, immunity, blood and circulation.

Cherries – a host of properties including anti-cancer, immunity, antioxidant and detoxifier, and benefit nervous system, heart and digestion.

Kiwis – one kiwi contains more Vitamin C than an orange. Aid eyesight, digestion, heart, immunity, and have anti-cancer properties.

Oranges – very high in Vitamin C, to ward off sickness and strengthen immunities. Also good for digestion, anti-cancer, detoxifying and heart.

Pears – especially good for the digestive system when the body is out of kilter. Also good for bones and immunity.

Watermelons – considered one of the best sources of Vitamin C, which boosts immunities. They help the nervous system and heart as well.

Peaches – a huge source of Vitamin C for immunity and keeping bugs away. Excellent for digestion, heart, eyes and nervous system.

Apples – best known for their detoxifying and digestive capabilities due to the pectin they contain. Other benefits include anti-inflammatory, heart, antioxidant and immunity.

Grapes – very rich in antioxidants – the red grapes contain more than the green. Very good for heart and for detoxifying liver and kidneys.

Apricots – bursting with iron, fresh or dried apricots are supreme brain food. Important for detoxifying, antioxidants, anti-cancer, digestion, nervous system, eyes and skin.

Plums – best known for their fibre, plums aid digestion. Also vital for blood, circulation, anti-cancer, bones and immunity.

Avocados – one of the best sources of Vitamin E for skin and immunity. Also help eyesight and hormones, and are an antioxidant.

Vegetables

Add to sandwiches, salads and dips, or use as a snack.

Carrots – one carrot can supply an entire day's beta-carotene, which strengthens eyes. It is a star-rated vegetable, assisting digestion, immunity, blood and circulation, nervous system, skin and hair.

Spinach – best noted for its iron and calcium to improve bones and teeth; it is also good for the heart and eyes, and contains antioxidants and anti-cancer properties.

Sweet peppers – the red, yellow or orange peppers have more beta-carotene (eyes) than the green and all have strong Vitamin C for immunity. Also assist bones, digestive system and heart.

Broccoli – a mammoth 'superfood' that is strong in antioxidants and anti-cancer properties. It is one of the richest sources of calcium for bones, and aids heart and digestion.

Peas – a very likeable children's vegetable. They are essential for improving heart, eyesight, digestion and immunity.

Sweetcorn – another favourite with children, corn is good for energy and fibre, but also first-rate for digestion, heart, blood, immunity, hormones and nervous system.

Asparagus – fantastic for flushing toxins out of body and assisting the digestive system, heart, blood and circulation. Big antioxidant and anti-cancer agent.

Green beans – fibre-rich vegetable which aids the heart and has a wealth of anti-cancer nutrients.

Beetroot – rich in iron to help blood, heart and circulation, but also hosts other advantages including detoxifying, antioxidant, anti-cancer and fighting sickness.

Cabbage – considered a 'star food' for its cumulative health gains: bones, blood and circulation, digestive and respiratory. Try it in wraps with lamb or chicken.

Celery – not a 'superfood' but is reputed to be good for sore throats because of its antiseptic qualities. Very good for bones, kidneys and bladder, and immunity.

Tomatoes – one of the easiest fruits or vegetables to get into a sandwich or salad. Very high in Vitamin C, so beneficial for immunity and warding off sickness. The lycopene they contain protects against cancer and also has Vitamin E for skin.

Courgettes – Not a 'superfood' but good for immunity, the nervous and digestive systems, and also aids eyesight.

Watercress – very potent antioxidant

and anti-cancer agent and provides other rewards including detoxifying, warding off sickness and aiding the heart.

Rocket – has so many more nutrients (and much more taste) than average lettuce. Contains high levels of Vitamin C for immunity, sickness prevention and also potent for anti-cancer, digestion and detoxifying.

Cucumber – not a 'superfood' but very good for digestion and bones, and has Vitamin C for sickness prevention. Try to eat with skins on whenever possible.

Salt

Should you use salt in children's food? The British Food Standards Agency states that the following recommendations apply:

Children under 5 – no salt

Age 6–7 – can have up to 3 grams per day

Age 7–10 – can have up to 5 grams per day

Age 11 and up – can have up to 6 grams per day

(6 grams is about 1 teaspoon)

It is vital to read labels and packets of prepared food to understand the level of salt. Processed food is notorious for having a lot of sodium, so the less you buy, the better. If you make it yourself you can control the quantities. Too much salt in a child's diet can cause heart and blood problems later in life, so it is advised to keep it minimal. That is not to say salt is entirely evil – it has iodine benefits and enhances the taste of food. It should be used in the early stages of cooking (in the water to boil pasta, sautéing onions, etc.) and for seasoning salads, but not sprinkled liberally over food. You want your food to taste good, so a little pinch used in the preparation is OK, but you need to consider what amounts are in the other foods that are purchased as well.

Sugar

It's fine for children to have some sugar but IN MODERATION. Sweets are part of childhood and we don't want to rob them of their fun. Too much, though, can cause adult diabetes and potentially make them fat. The most immediate (and annoying) effect is the wild mood swings, hyperactivity and aggressive behaviour it causes. Processed snacks, 'juice' drinks and soft drinks are the worst sources of high sugars. Read the label and if you see sugar listed as one of the first three ingredients, then you know it's bad. Sugar goes by many names – glucose, dextrose, corn syrup, maltose, lactose, molasses, brown sugar and sugar syrup, to name just a few.

Fat

Children NEED to eat fat for development of hormones, the brain and nervous system. I wish we could say the same for adults! There are two types of fat they require: essential fatty acids and saturated fats. The first are Omega-3 and Omega-6, derived from nuts, seeds, oily fish and wholegrains, and they are the good sort. The latter are derived from red meat, poultry and dairy products. Kids still need these, but not enormous amounts. Watch out for hydrogenated oil, which is chemically treated vegetable oil that is converted into solid fat. It is used in a lot of processed foods like crisps. If they eat too much of the bad kind, it can block the absorption of the good ones. Try to use olive oil or pure vegetable oil whenever cooking for children.

A week's lunch plan and shopping list

Making lunches is far less stressful if you take ten minutes to figure out what you are making for the week. You can buy everything at once on your weekly shop.

A few bits of advice

Size – don't put too much food in or it will go to waste. Most kids eat in short shifts and have very little time to eat their packed lunch. Peel or cut up fruit when possible.

Containers – use disposable bags for sandwiches and fruit, and plastic sealable containers for salads. Hot soups or stews should be packed in an insulated flask.

Lunch boxes – soft padded insulated lunch boxes are recommended for keeping food fresh. Freeze a tub of yogurt or chill a small juice box to add additional cooling. Little freezer packs can be used as well.

Bread – vary the bread as much as you can. Use baguettes, rolls or bagels shortly after you buy them. They go stale faster than normal bread. Freeze leftovers if not using within a couple of days. Try to buy 'grainy' or at least wholemeal, versus white, sliced bread if possible.

Each day you should try to pack the following:
Main – sandwich, cheese and crackers, soup, salad or dip with crudités
Fruit – a couple of pieces of their favourite, like berries, apple pieces, bananas, etc.
Snack or treat – real fruit breakfast bars, popcorn, pretzels, fromage frais, etc. Once a week, pack something wicked like a brownie, crisps or a chocolate fairy cake.
Drinks – avoid boxes of juice which say 'juice drink'. This means sugar is added. Stick with water or pure juice. A small reusable water bottle is very economical.

Menu

Monday
Salami, rocket and
tomato baguette
Small bottle of water
Parmesan popcorn
Handful of mixed
berries

Tuesday
Turkey, cheese and
apple bagel
Box of juice
Real fruit breakfast
bar
Small clementine or
half an orange,
peeled

Wednesday
Corkscrew pasta with
tuna, mayonnaise and
celery
Small bottle of water
Bag of chocolate-
covered raisins
Peeled and sliced
kiwi

Thursday
Corkscrew pasta with
tuna, mayonnaise and
celery
Tub of fromage frais
with fruit
Chocolate-dipped
strawberries
Box of juice

Friday
Hummus with
breadsticks, carrot
and celery sticks
Small bottle of water
Brownies with white
chocolate chunks
Half an apple, cut
into pieces

Shopping list

Some of these items might exist already in your cupboards or fridge.

Fruit
Apples
Strawberries
Blueberries
Oranges
Kiwi
Avocado – it's actually
a fruit, not a
vegetable
Cherry tomatoes –
these are also fruit,
not vegetables

Vegetables
Cucumber
Rocket
Carrots
Celery

Meat
Slices of turkey from
deli counter
Pack of sliced salami

Dairy
Slices of cheese
Parmesan
Tubs of fromage frais

Other
Bagels
Popping corn
Olives
Small bottles of water
Juice boxes
Mayonnaise
Tin of tuna
Real fruit breakfast
bars
Chocolate-covered
raisins
Small baguettes

Tub of hummus
Breadsticks
Bars of baking
chocolate – white,
milk and plain
Eggs
Pasta (of various
shapes – ask your
kids which they
prefer)

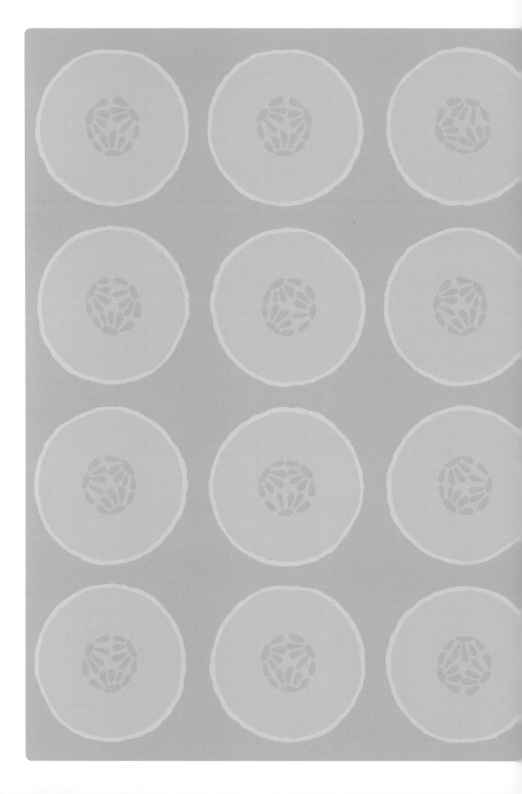

Sandwiches, wraps and rolls

Helpful sandwich ingredients to stock in your fridge and cupboard from week to week.

Meats and fish

- Deli whole roasted chicken
- Salami – chorizo, French, Italian
- Ham
- Sliced turkey (real, not pressed)
- Smoked salmon
- Bacon (already cooked)

Cheeses

- Cream cheese
- Sliced cheese – Cheddar, Swiss, Gruyère
- Block or hard cheese such as mild Cheddar
- Feta

Cupboard and fridge

- Peanut butter
- Jam
- Marmite
- Mayonnaise
- Butter
- Salsa
- Hummus
- Mustard

Breads

- Flour tortilla (also known as wraps)
- French baguettes (you can freeze any remaining portions)
- Soft rolls
- Croissants
- Pitta
- Seeded white or brown sliced bread

Vegetables

- Carrots
- Cucumbers
- Lettuce – iceberg, Little Gem, spinach, rocket, etc.
- Tomatoes
- Avocados

Buy a roast chicken at the deli counter and use the meat to create a week's worth of salads and sandwiches. It beats the processed chicken slices sold in packs.

Chicken taco wrap

- ◆ 1 tortilla
- ◆ 1 handful chopped roasted chicken or leftover beef
- ◆ 2 tbsp grated Cheddar cheese
- ◆ 2 cherry tomatoes, cut into quarters
- ◆ 1 tbsp of your favourite mild salsa

Heat the tortilla for two seconds in the microwave and it will be easier to wrap. Place all of the filling in the centre of the tortilla. Fold the sides in first and then roll it up as tightly as possible.

Adventurous tastes
red onions, coriander leaves, chilli powder sprinkled on the chicken

Milder tastes
omit the salsa, add chopped lettuce or avocado

You can buy already-cooked bacon at supermarkets or use leftovers from breakfast. Streaky is preferable to back bacon, as it tastes better cold and is crispier.

Avocado, bacon and cream cheese baguette

- Half a small baguette, split open
- 1 tbsp cream cheese
- 3 slices avocado
- 2–3 rashers cooked streaky bacon

Spread the bread with the cream cheese and then place the avocado and bacon on top.

Adventurous tastes

mild goat's cheese instead of cream cheese. Add spinach or rocket leaves

Milder tastes

use lettuce or tomato instead of avocado. Cheddar, mayonnaise or butter to replace cream cheese

To avoid your child becoming a social pariah with an over-fragrant lunch box, pack a frozen juice or yogurt to keep it icy cold and smelling fresh.

Smoked salmon, tomato and cream cheese bagels

◆ 1 bagel, sliced in half
◆ 2 slices smoked salmon
◆ 2 tbsp cream cheese
◆ 1 slice tomato

Spread the bagel with cream cheese and add the other ingredients. Wrap in parchment paper and then place in a bag.

Adventurous tastes
chopped dill or red onion

Milder tastes
replace salmon with cucumber

Open any lunch box in Britain and you may very well find a ham and cheese sandwich. If your child won't eat anything else, try changing the bread.

Ham and cheese sandwich

◆ Seeded white or brown bread, soft roll, croissant or baguette
◆ 2 slices thick ham
◆ 1 slice cheese – Swiss, Gruyère or Cheddar
◆ Butter or mayonnaise

Spread the butter or mayonnaise on the bread and add the other ingredients.

Adventurous tastes

add pickles, English mustard, replace ham with prosciutto, red onion slices

Milder tastes

add crunchy iceberg lettuce, cucumbers or slice of tomato

Save leftover sausages from tea and use them in sandwiches. Be sure to use brands with a high percentage of meat, which taste better cold.

Cold sausage sandwich

- Soft seeded white or brown roll, baguette or pitta pocket
- 1–2 cooked sausages, split lengthways (chipolata, pork, Italian)
- Small handful lettuce
- Spoonful of ketchup or brown sauce

Spread the bread with ketchup. Add the sausages and lettuce. Top with bread and press together.

Adventurous tastes

slice of raw or roasted red pepper (from jar), rocket, mustard

Health incentive

ketchup isn't as bad as you think – when tomatoes are cooked they release more lycopene, a powerful anti-cancer agent and immune system booster

This is a great way to use up leftovers from a Sunday roast. It makes a great change from ham.

Beef and tomato sandwich

- ◆ 1 soft white or brown roll
- ◆ 1 slice roast beef
- ◆ 2 leaves iceberg lettuce
- ◆ 1 thickly sliced tomato
- ◆ 1 tbsp mayonnaise or salad cream

Spread the mayonnaise on the roll and fill with other ingredients.

Adventurous tastes

add watercress, rocket, horseradish cream, mustard, or chunks of Gorgonzola cheese

Health incentive

beef is a great source of protein, B vitamins (immunity) and iron, which is important for healthy blood. Keep building muscle on those skinny arms and legs

Thinly sliced chorizo is sold in the salami section of most supermarkets and, surprisingly, most children really like the taste of it.

Chorizo sandwiches

◆ Seeded white or brown bread, soft rolls or baguettes
◆ 4 pieces thinly sliced chorizo salami
◆ 1 small handful of rocket or lettuce
◆ Mayonnaise or butter

Spread the mayonnaise or butter on the bread. Add the chorizo and tomato, and press together.

Adventurous tastes

cornichon pickles, watercress

Milder tastes

ham or other salami, replace rocket with Little Gem lettuce

Health incentive

wherever possible, try adding rocket into a sandwich. It's full of Vitamin C, for keeping bugs at bay, and beta-carotene, which strengthens eyesight

Lettuce with darker colours means more nutrients. It also has a better flavour than soggy, bog-standard lettuce

By using a tortilla wrap to seal this sandwich, the potential of wafting 'egg odour' can be eliminated. Again, use a frozen juice box or yogurt to keep everything fresh.

Tuna, egg and lettuce wrap

◆ 1 tortilla
◆ ½ tin tuna, drained
◆ 1 tbsp mayonnaise or salad cream
◆ 1 hard-boiled egg, sliced
◆ Little Gem lettuce

Warm the tortilla for two seconds in microwave to soften. Mix the tuna with the mayonnaise and place in the middle of the tortilla. Place the egg slices over and top with lettuce. Bring the sides in and roll up tightly.

Adventurous tastes
use watercress, rocket or spinach

Milder tastes
replace egg with sweetcorn

Mozzarella meets one of the 'CSS' taste criteria (creamy, salty or sweet), and is a welcome change from mild Cheddar.

Ham, tomato and fresh mozzarella roll

- ◆ Crusty seeded roll, baguette or soft roll
- ◆ Butter or mayonnaise
- ◆ 1–2 slices of ham
- ◆ 2 slices fresh mozzarella
- ◆ 2 slices of tomato

Spread the bread with butter or mayonnaise, add the ham, tomato and mozzarella.

Adventurous tastes

replace mayonnaise with pesto, slices of raw red pepper, rocket or basil leaves

Milder tastes

replace mozzarella with Cheddar cheese

Of course, your child has to be keen on fish to pack this. Kids normally show a pretty extreme reaction to fish . . . they love it or loathe it. The smoked flavour masks its fishiness. Try the tasty packs of fillets sprinkled with pepper.

Smoked trout, cheese and crackers

- ◆ 4 seeded crackers
- ◆ 1 small piece of flaky smoked trout or mackerel
- ◆ 2 small chunks of mild cheese like Cheddar
- ◆ Small bunch of green grapes

Wrap the fish in parchment paper and then place in a bag. This will keep it smelling fresh. Wrap the others in a plastic bag.

Adventurous tastes

replace fish with salami, chicken or just cheese

Health incentive

oily fish like mackerel is considered one of the most potent foods you can eat. Besides Omega-3 fats and Vitamin D, it's also reputed to improve brain function and concentration due to the B vitamins . . . could be helpful when they are doing their homework

Even if your kids aren't bean lovers, try creamy cannellini.
Put them in the bottom of the pitta so their classmates don't
see . . . conformity means a lot.

Salami, bean and Parmesan pitta

- ◆ 1 pitta bread with top cut open (or use a tortilla)
- ◆ 2 tbsp drained tinned cannellini beans
- ◆ 2–3 slices any salami
- ◆ 3 cherry tomatoes, halved
- ◆ 2 tbsp Parmesan, grated on large holes
- ◆ 1 tbsp salad cream

Fill the pitta with the beans and salad cream, then top
with the Parmesan, cherry tomatoes and salami.

Adventurous tastes

*add rocket, spinach, raw red
pepper slices or olives*

Milder tastes

*replace beans with
cucumbers, replace salami
with ham*

I am always amazed (and happy) that most kids will gladly eat hummus. If they knew it was chickpeas they might change their minds.

Hummus pitta with veggies

◆ 1 pitta bread with top cut open
◆ 2 tbsp hummus
◆ Half a carrot, peeled and grated
◆ 3 slices cucumber
◆ 2–3 small strips of red peppers

Open the pitta and add the hummus first, followed by the vegetables.

Adventurous tastes
add some chunks of feta, rocket or spring onion

Milder tastes
omit peppers and replace with lettuce

It's always worth trying something different, and tandoori chicken could well be a winner. Mango chutney is sweet . . . so it just might be popular.

Tandoori chicken pitta

- ◆ 1 pitta bread with top cut open
- ◆ 2 strips store-bought tandoori chicken
- ◆ Iceberg lettuce
- ◆ 3 slices cucumber
- ◆ 1 tbsp plain yogurt

Place the chicken, lettuce and cucumber in the pitta and top with the yogurt.

Adventurous tastes
add mango chutney, chopped spring onion, mint

Milder tastes
replace tandoori with normal roast chicken

This is another good one for leftovers from Sunday lunch. Pork would be delicious as well.

Lamb kebab wrap

- ◆ 1 tortilla, Middle Eastern flatbread or pitta bread
- ◆ 3 pieces roast lamb
- ◆ 3 slices cucumber
- ◆ 3 cherry tomatoes, halved
- ◆ 1 tbsp mayonnaise, yogurt, salad cream or even hummus

Place the lamb, cucumber, tomatoes and mayonnaise in the middle of the tortilla. Roll the sides in first and then roll up the bottom. Secure with a toothpick.

Adventurous tastes

spring onions, shredded raw cabbage, coriander

Milder tastes

use chicken or cheese instead of lamb

This is a great classic, which can be embellished depending on taste buds.

Egg salad sandwich

(Makes enough for two sandwiches – filling will last two days, refrigerated)
- ◆ Seeded brown or white bread, roll or baguette
- ◆ 3 hard-boiled eggs, cooled, peeled and diced
- ◆ 3 tbsp mayonnaise

Mix together the eggs and mayonnaise, and spread liberally on the bread to make a sandwich, or in the roll or baguette.

Adventurous tastes

add cress, watercress, spinach, thin beef, smoked salmon

Milder tastes

add ham or iceberg lettuce

Feta makes a good sandwich filling, as it's mild, creamy and salty. To avoid waste, buy it in jars packed in olive oil and use as much as you need.

Feta, tomato and cucumber baguette

- ◆ Half a small baguette, halved lengthways
- ◆ 4 small cubes of feta
- ◆ 3 cherry tomatoes, halved
- ◆ Small chunk cubed or sliced cucumber
- ◆ Mayonnaise or butter

Spread the bread with butter or mayonnaise, add the tomatoes and cucumber, and crumble the feta over them.

Adventurous tastes
replace mayonnaise with a little red vinegar and oil, fresh mint or dill, red onion

Milder tastes
replace feta with mild Cheddar or spread with cream cheese

Some children want only the fillings, and are not so keen on the bread. It's a promising sign of a foodie.

The deli bag – ham, cheese and crackers

- 2–3 breadsticks or crackers
- 1 slice ham, rolled up
- 4 cherry tomatoes
- 2–3 slices salami
- 1 piece favourite cheese

Pack all of the ingredients separately, and your child can 'mix and match'.

Adventurous tastes

pitted olives, cubes of feta cheese, grapes

Buy sliced turkey from the deli. The packets of 'pressed', or processed, meat are far from the real thing . . . quite scary really.

Turkey, cheese and apple bagel

◆ 1 bagel, sliced lengthways
◆ 2 pieces turkey
◆ 4 thin slices apple
◆ 1 slice of cheese
◆ Mayonnaise or butter

Spread the bagel halves with mayonnaise or butter and stack apple, turkey and cheese inside.

Adventurous tastes

a little chutney, pickles, mustard

Health incentive

turkey is full protein and contains all three of the B vitamins – which help the nervous system (think concentration and brainpower)

Some supermarkets sell meatballs formed, rolled and uncooked. Pan-fry a few for tea and save some for lunches.

Cold meatball pitta

◆ 1 pitta bread with top cut open
◆ 2 cooked meatballs
◆ 2 pieces crisp lettuce
◆ 1 slice tomato
◆ Ketchup

Place the meatballs, lettuce and tomato in the pitta and squirt in a bit of ketchup.

Adventurous tastes
brown sauce, thin slices of red onion, pickles

Milder tastes
use butter in place of ketchup, luncheon meat instead of meatballs

Again, streaky bacon is best for this, cooking up thin
and flaky.

Bacon, lettuce and tomato sandwich

◆ Toasted seeded white or brown bread
◆ 2 rashers cooked bacon
◆ 1 slice tomato
◆ 2 leaves iceberg or Little Gem lettuce
◆ Mayonnaise

Spread the bread with the mayonnaise and layer the
bacon, lettuce and tomato on top. Press together and
cut into halves.

Adventurous tastes
*rocket, watercress or
spinach instead of iceberg*

Milder tastes
butter instead of mayonnaise

Small prawns have a sweet taste and aren't too expensive either.

Pitta with prawn and celery salad

◆ Pitta pocket, sliced open, or soft roll
◆ 1 small handful tiny cooked prawns
◆ 1 tbsp mayonnaise
◆ 1 tbsp ketchup
◆ Half a stick of celery, diced

Mix the prawns, mayonnaise, ketchup and celery in a bowl. Stuff the mixture in to a pitta or soft roll with the lettuce.

Adventurous tastes

use a pinch of curry powder to replace ketchup, rocket, spinach or watercress

Health incentives

prawns have a large concentration of nutrients that boost immunity and protect against sickness. They are among the few

foods with natural iodine, which is vital for your metabolism (salt in crisps doesn't count)

Try to sneak the watercress into this one . . . you never know unless you try.

Tomato, watercress and salad cream sandwich

◆ Thick-sliced and toasted seeded white or brown bread
◆ 2 thick slices of beef tomato
◆ Small handful watercress leaves
◆ Salad cream or mayonnaise

Spread the salad cream over the toasted bread. Layer the cress and tomatoes on top and press together. Cut in half.

Adventurous tastes

thinly sliced beef, thinly sliced red onion

Health incentive

watercress is considered one of the 'superfoods'. Besides containing antioxidants and calcium, it is a great detoxifier (maybe it will help balance out the many bags of crisps that get consumed)

You need to quickly grill halloumi to give it flavour, and thereafter it tastes good hot or cold. It's a great source of protein for vegetarians.

Grilled halloumi, tomato and cucumber baguette

- ◆ Half a small baguette or crusty roll
- ◆ 2 slices halloumi cheese
- ◆ 3 slices cucumber
- ◆ 1 sliced tomato
- ◆ Mayonnaise or butter
- ◆ Crunchy lettuce

Griddle the halloumi until it has black marks on both sides (pan-frying works too). Spread the butter or mayonnaise on the baguette and layer the halloumi, cucumber, tomato and lettuce. Press shut and cut in half.

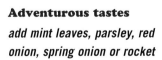

Adventurous tastes	**Milder tastes**
add mint leaves, parsley, red onion, spring onion or rocket	*other mild cheese like Swiss, Emmental or Gruyère*

Not all schools are nut free, especially secondary schools. Peanut butter is fantastic because it's so easy and healthy. So if you're able to . . . go for it.

Peanut butter and jam sandwich

◆ White or brown seeded bread
◆ Your favourite peanut butter
◆ Your favourite jam

Spread the bread as thickly as you like with peanut butter and then put a thin layer of jam on top. Press the bread together and cut in half.

Adventurous tastes
add banana or apple slices

Milder tastes
just do peanut butter on its own

You can buy chicken satay pieces already marinated and cooked at most supermarkets, so choose your favourite.

Chicken satay baguette

◆ Half a baguette, sliced, or other favourite bread
◆ 2–3 chicken satay pieces
◆ 2–3 cucumber slices
◆ 2 tbsp grated carrot
◆ Mayonnaise

Spread the baguette with mayonnaise and layer the chicken, cucumbers and carrot on top. Press together.

Adventurous tastes
sweet chilli dipping sauce, prepared peanut sauce (if you are allowed), fresh coriander

Milder tastes
use regular roast chicken

Fruit and cheese are a nice combination and a good meatless option.

Seeded roll with Cheddar, pear and chutney

- ◆ 1 seeded roll, baguette or croissant, split in half
- ◆ 1 thick slice of mild Cheddar
- ◆ 2–3 slices pear
- ◆ 1 tbsp mild chutney

Spread the bread with the chutney and layer the Cheddar and pear on top. Press together and cut in half.

Adventurous tastes

use stronger Cheddar or brie

Milder tastes

use butter instead of chutney, or apple in place of pear

This is a mild version of a chicken Caesar salad wrap – but no one needs to know.

Chicken salad wrap

- ◆ 1 tortilla
- ◆ 2–3 pieces roasted chicken
- ◆ 3–4 croutons
- ◆ 2–3 leaves Little Gem lettuce
- ◆ 1 tbsp Caesar salad dressing (Pizza Express one is good)

Heat the tortilla for two seconds in the microwave and then place all of the filling in the middle. Bring the sides in first and then roll up.

Other good additions
halved cherry tomatoes or cooked bacon

Favourites like this are always a good opportunity for slipping in a few vegetables or lettuce.

Tuna, sweetcorn and spinach roll

◆ Brown or white seeded bread or soft seeded roll
◆ Half a tin of tuna
◆ 2 tbsp mayonnaise
◆ 2 tbsp tinned sweetcorn
◆ Small handful of baby spinach

Mix the tuna with the sweetcorn and mayonnaise. Spread on the roll and top with the spinach.

Other good additions

rings of raw red pepper, shredded carrots, tomatoes

Health incentive

try to get spinach in whenever you can – it hosts a whopping source of vitamins . . . C, B2, B3, calcium and E to name a few. Cooking destroys its Vitamin C, so raw is best

An oldie but a goody.

Marmite on toast

- ◆ White or brown seeded bread
- ◆ 1 tsp Marmite
- ◆ Butter

Toast the bread, spread the butter over and then the Marmite.

Cornichons seem like a great way to introduce your kids to pickles. Who couldn't love their miniature size? Mine picked them all out and I found the remnants at the bottom of the lunch box. I didn't despair because the following week they asked for them . . . go figure.

French salami and pickle baguette

◆ Half a small baguette, split in half
◆ 4 slices French salami
◆ 4–5 cornichon pickles
◆ Butter or mayonnaise

Spread the butter on the baguette and add the salami and pickles.

Adventurous tastes
mustard or rocket

Milder tastes
OK, take the pickles off!

Please don't be put off by the suggestion that you should put chilli sauce on your child's sandwich, as some kids really do like it. Used in small quantities, it's not even hot and it's incredibly sweet . . . hence the attraction.

Roast chicken baguette with sweet chilli dipping sauce

◆ Half a French baguette, a tortilla wrap or a crusty roll
◆ 1 large handful of roasted chicken (use supermarket ready-roasted if you prefer)
◆ 1 tbsp sweet chilli dipping sauce
◆ 2–3 pieces of Little Gem lettuce
◆ 2–3 slices cucumber

Place all ingredients in the bread and drizzle the chilli sauce over. Press together.

Milder tastes

use bottled barbeque sauce instead of sweet chilli dipping sauce

Curry is probably one of the first 'exotic' foods that children experience. It seems to appeal greatly, so give it a try. The sultanas are up to you . . . some children have amazing radar to retrieve them from any food.

Coronation chicken salad pitta

◆ Pitta bread with top cut open
◆ 2 small handfuls chopped chicken
◆ 1 tsp mild curry powder
◆ 3 tbsp of mayonnaise or yogurt
◆ 1 tbsp sultanas – optional

In a small bowl, mix together the chicken, curry powder and yogurt. Stuff into the pitta and add sultanas if required.

Adventurous tastes

top with some halved seedless grapes

This is an American creation which uses very soft long rolls stuffed with stacks of salami and cheese. Children really love them and so do adults. This is a simplified version.

Submarine sandwich

- ◆ Soft white submarine rolls or white rolls
- ◆ 4 slices of your favourite salami (pepperoni, Milano, French or German)
- ◆ 4 slices of your favourite cheese
- ◆ Sliced tomato
- ◆ Mayonnaise

Spread the mayonnaise on the roll. Layer the salami, cheese and tomato and press together.

Adventurous tastes

chopped gherkins or sweet pickled peppers, red onions, vinegar and oil, cheese such as provolone or Gruyère

Milder tastes

Replace mayonnaise with butter

Snacks and dips

Dips with crudités can be a refreshing and filling alternative
to sandwiches. Some of these will need to be made ahead
and others can be quickly assembled on the day. Here is a
list of healthy, handy snacks to keep in your store cupboard.

Things to buy

- ◆ Pretzels (much healthier than crisps)
- ◆ Sunflower seeds
- ◆ Raisins
- ◆ Dried fruit
- ◆ Vegetable crisps
- ◆ Unshelled pistachios (if you are allowed)
- ◆ Soy nuts
- ◆ Pumpkin seeds
- ◆ Breadsticks
- ◆ Breakfast fruit bars (the ones that actually have fruit
  in them)
- ◆ Yogurt tubs
- ◆ Pitted olives
- ◆ Twiglets (not so bad)

Of course you can buy very good hummus, but it can get expensive if your kids really like it. My two boys can demolish one small tub for a snack, so if I have time, I make it.

Hummus

- 400g/14oz tin of chickpeas
- Juice of 2 lemons
- 125ml/4fl oz tahini
- 3 garlic cloves, crushed
- ½ tsp salt
- 4 tbsp olive oil

A blender works best for this. Purée the chickpeas with their liquid and add the lemon juice, tahini, garlic, salt and olive oil. Taste for additional salt and lemon. This keeps for one week, refrigerated. Pack in small containers with your favourite crudités – carrots, celery, cucumber, sugarsnap peas or tomatoes.

Popcorn is easy to make at home and doesn't have copious amounts of hydrogenated fats (like the sort you buy in paper boxes to cook in the microwave). Try other flavourings like mild chilli powder.

Parmesan popcorn

- ◆ 150g/5oz popping corn
- ◆ 90ml/3fl oz vegetable oil
- ◆ 30g/1oz grated Parmesan

Use an old heavy pot and heat the vegetable oil and popcorn on medium heat. Place a lid on top and let the corn pop until you don't hear it any more. Immediately remove from the heat and sprinkle with the Parmesan. This will keep for three days in an airtight container.

If your child has stronger tastes, add some chopped herbs or a little sweet chilli dipping sauce to the cream cheese . . . You might be surprised – remember, 'CSS' (creamy, sweet, salty).

Cream cheese with sugarsnap peas

◆ 100g/3½oz cream cheese
◆ A handful of sugarsnap peas or celery sticks

Pack the cream cheese in a small container with the vegetables.

If asparagus isn't tolerated then try wrapping ham around a different vegetable like carrot sticks.

Asparagus and ham roll-ups

◆ 2 spears of asparagus, trimmed
◆ 2 slices ham

Boil, microwave or grill the asparagus for one to two minutes. It doesn't take long and should be *al dente*. If boiling or steaming, rinse in cold water, dry, and then roll up each one in the ham.

**Who needs to know this is beans? Just call it 'white dip'.
Beans are a great source of protein, fibre and calcium.**

White bean, honey and rosemary dip with breadsticks

- ◆ 400g/14oz tin cannellini or other creamy beans, drained
- ◆ 1 tbsp honey
- ◆ 1 tsp fresh rosemary, chopped
- ◆ 1 clove garlic, crushed
- ◆ ½ tsp salt
- ◆ 2 tbsp olive oil
- ◆ Juice of half a lemon

Purée all of the ingredients in a blender or food processor. Add some water if the mixture is too thick. This keeps for one week, refrigerated. Pack a small container with breadsticks or crudités.

Greek yogurt is thick and creamy without being too sour, so it appeals more to young palates. Add a clove of crushed garlic if you're allowed.

Tzatziki dip with cucumbers

◆ Half a medium cucumber peeled, seeded and grated
◆ Salt
◆ 200g/7oz Greek yogurt (Total brand is good)
◆ 1 tbsp fresh dill or mint, chopped

Place the cucumbers in a colander and mix with the salt. Leave for thirty minutes to drain and then mix with the other ingredients. Keeps for four days, refrigerated. Pack in a small container with cucumber sticks or other crudités.

Health incentive
yogurt is packed with calcium and generates good bacteria for stomachs

Ask your child whether it's politically acceptable to have pink food at school. Barbie enthusiasts could be good candidates.

Beetroot dip with Parmesan

- ◆ 2 small beetroots
- ◆ 1 clove garlic
- ◆ 2 tbsp olive oil
- ◆ 100g/3½oz pine nuts, toasted and cooled
- ◆ 30g/1oz thick-grated Parmesan cheese
- ◆ 60ml/2fl oz extra virgin olive oil

Purée the beetroot and garlic in a food processor or blender. Add the nuts, Parmesan and oil and pulse a couple of times to keep crunchy. Season with salt and pepper. It will keep refrigerated for one week. Pack a small container with some pitta bread cut into triangles or crudités.

Note: Be aware this has nuts, so only use if allowed.

Health incentive

beetroots are rich in Vitamin C, calcium and iron, but most importantly they boost immunity, detoxify and clean your blood. Just remember to warn your child that their wee will turn pink and that they're not dying from a fatal disease

It will surprise you how much children love this, but it's probably due to its sweet and sour nature. This is also very good in wraps or pittas.

Tangy red bean dip

- ◆ 1 tbsp olive oil
- ◆ 1 medium onion, chopped
- ◆ 1 garlic clove, chopped
- ◆ 400g/14oz tin kidney beans, drained
- ◆ 75ml/2fl oz cider vinegar
- ◆ 4 tbsp honey
- ◆ ½ tsp each of mild chilli powder, cumin and salt

Heat the olive oil in a medium pan. Add the onion, garlic and salt. Sauté for four minutes and then add the beans. Stir in the vinegar, honey, chilli powder and cumin. Simmer over a low heat for about five minutes, stirring occasionally. Purée in a food processor. Serve with tortilla chips or crudités.

Guacamole needs to be made fresh: the shop-bought version is truly disgusting and full of preservatives.

Quick guacamole with crudités

◆ 2 ripe avocados, peeled and pitted
◆ Juice of one lemon
◆ Salt
◆ 1 tbsp Worcestershire sauce
◆ Half a clove of garlic, crushed

Crush all of the ingredients with a potato masher or purée in a food processor. Pack a small container with vegetable sticks or a few tortilla chips. This keeps for one day, refrigerated, but keep plastic wrap directly on surface to keep it from turning brown.

Health incentives

considered one of the top ten healthy fruits, avocados do contain fat but the good kind (children actually need fat in their diet anyway) and promote good skin and shiny hair

These will appear to be a treat but are actually pretty healthy.

Apricot and cream cheese celery sticks

◆ 2 ready-soaked dried apricots
◆ 6 tbsp cream cheese
◆ 2 sticks celery, trimmed

Purée the apricots with the cream cheese and then spread on the celery sticks. Cut into smaller pieces and pack in a container or bag

Who could blame children for not wanting to eat plain sunflower seeds? They are pretty boring, but add some salt and oil and they are transformed. You can also buy them prepared this way.

Toasted sunflower seeds

◆ A little olive oil
◆ 100g/3½oz sunflower seeds
◆ Salt

Heat the oil and sunflower seeds in a non-stick frying pan. Toast them over a medium-to-low heat until slightly browned, about two minutes. Sprinkle with salt and tip into a bowl. These keep fresh in a sealed container for one week.

Health incentive

sunflower seeds are one of the most perfect foods your child can eat, containing Vitamins A, B, D, E, K, calcium and anti-cancer properties, to name just a few

The adults in the house might eat these before the children ever get to them. Older children, whose schools usually don't have nut bans, would be good candidates for these.

Soy and sesame nuts

◆ 200g/7oz walnuts and pecans
◆ 1 tbsp sesame seeds – white and/or black
◆ 5 tbsp honey
◆ 3 tbsp caster sugar
◆ 2 tsp soy sauce
◆ 1 tbsp olive oil

Preheat the oven to 200°C, gas mark 6. Mix all of the ingredients together in a small bowl. Line a baking sheet with silicone-treated baking paper and add the nut mixture. Bake for four to five minutes until toasted. Remove the paper with the nuts from the baking sheet and let cool. Store in a glass jar with a fitted lid and they will keep fresh for one week. Pack a small bag in lunch box.

Health incentive

Despite their outlawed status, nuts are still extremely important in children's diets and are a great source of protein, Vitamin E, calcium, iron and anti-cancer agents

The important thing about these is that, unlike processed 'cheesy biscuits', you know exactly what you are getting.

Cheddar penny biscuits

◆ 100g/3½oz plain flour
◆ 60g/2oz cold butter, diced
◆ 90g/3oz medium or mature Cheddar cheese, grated
◆ 1 egg

Preheat oven to 200°C, gas mark 6. Place the flour and butter in a food processor and pulse until the mixture resembles crumbs. Alternatively, you can do this by hand. Add the cheese and egg and mix until a dough forms. Roll the dough out to a thickness of 5mm/¼ inch and cut out small circles with a tiny pastry cutter or small shot glass. Place on a baking tray lined with parchment paper. Bake for eight minutes until golden. Cool on a rack.

These will keep in an airtight container for two weeks but I doubt they will last that long.

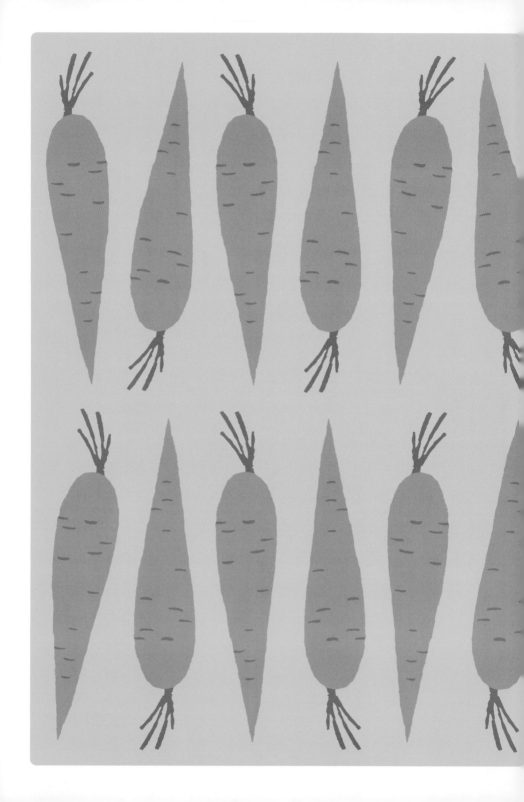

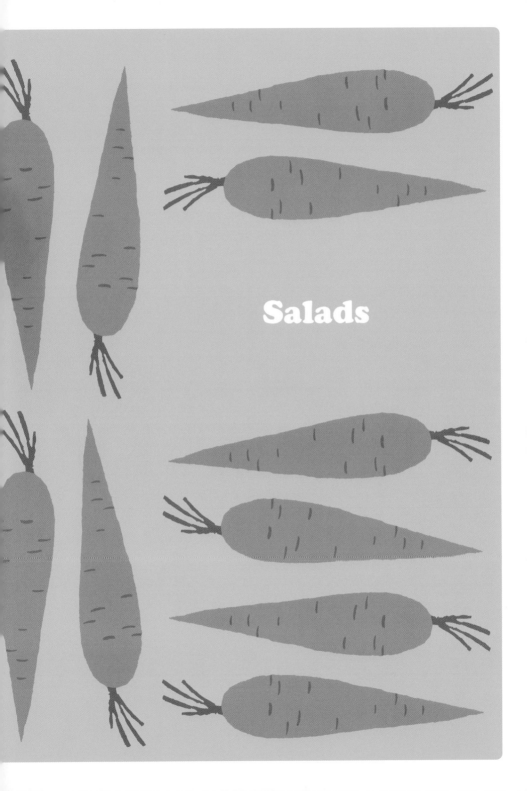

Salads

If you find your child likes a particular salad, then stick with it and slowly add a few more veggies to it every week. All of these will keep for three days, so make one a week for variety. The best way to pack these is in reusable containers with lids.

Things to stock up on

If you are short on time, don't feel guilty about buying prepared salads from good delis, organic food shops, your favourite supermarket or healthy lunch takeaways.

Cupboard essentials
Asian egg noodles
Pasta noodles
Vinegar and olive oil
Pesto
Tuna
Lentils
Couscous
Soy sauce
Tinned salmon
Sun-dried tomato paste

Cheese
Feta
Cheddar
Parmesan
Mozzarella

Meats
Salami
Ham
Roasted chicken

Vegetables
Carrots
Lettuce
Broccoli
Snow peas
Tomatoes
Cucumbers
Red peppers
Celery
Avocado

Try to buy a pesto that is made with olive oil rather than vegetable oil – the taste is much better. Delis usually carry home-made pesto, which is worth a special trip.

Broccoli pesto pasta with tomatoes

Makes 4 salads
- 250g/8oz rigatoni or other short pasta
- 2 handfuls broccoli florets
- 100ml/3½fl oz prepared pesto
- 1 tsp balsamic vinegar
- 4 cherry tomatoes, halved

Boil the pasta in salted water. When nearly done, add the broccoli and cook everything *al dente*. Drain, rinse in cold water and pour into a bowl. Add the pesto, vinegar and tomatoes and mix together. Refrigerate until needed. (Keeps for two days.)

The pasta aisle is my sons' favourite section of the supermarket, second only to cereal. With so many great shapes, let them choose their favourite.

Pasta with tuna, mayonnaise and celery

Makes 4 salads
- ◆ 250g/8oz fusilli or other short pasta
- ◆ 1 tin tuna, drained
- ◆ 4 tbsp mayonnaise
- ◆ 1 stick celery, finely diced

Boil the pasta in salted water until *al dente*. Drain and rinse with cold water. Place in a bowl and mix with the tuna, mayonnaise and celery. Refrigerate until needed. (Will keep for three days.)

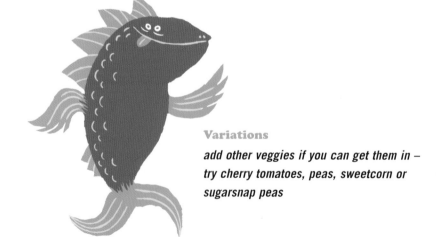

Variations

add other veggies if you can get them in – try cherry tomatoes, peas, sweetcorn or sugarsnap peas

A ripe avocado should be dark in colour and soft to the touch. It does pay sometimes to buy the 'ripe and ready' type just to be sure. A hard unripe one could put them off for ever.

Avocado, mozzarella, tomato and bacon

Makes 1 salad

◆ Half a small, ripe avocado, cut into chunks
◆ 4 cherry tomatoes, halved
◆ 3 small mozzarella balls (*bocconcini*)
◆ 1 cooked rasher of bacon, crumbled
◆ 1 tsp each of balsamic vinegar and olive oil or your favourite dressing

Place the ingredients in a container and pour the vinegar and oil over. Season with salt and pepper and seal well. Eat on the day.

Variations

use salad cream instead of vinegar and oil. Add sweetcorn, fresh basil or leave out the avocado

Cottage cheese is brilliant for salads and is usually well received. Buy them the full-fat variety, which tastes better.

Cottage cheese with ham and pineapple

Makes 1 salad
◆ 1 large scoop of your favourite cottage cheese
◆ 1 slice ham, cut into strips
◆ 4–5 chunks of pineapple (fresh if possible)

Arrange the ingredients in a container and seal. Keeps for two days in the fridge.

Variations

add chopped red pepper, grated carrots, cherry tomatoes or cooked peas

Try to get baby courgettes, which are sweeter than the big tough ones.

Pasta wheels with courgettes, lemon and basil

Makes 4 salads
- ◆ 250g/8oz wheel-shaped or other short pasta
- ◆ 6 baby courgettes, sliced into very thin coins
- ◆ Small handful of chopped fresh basil leaves
- ◆ Zest and juice of 1 lemon
- ◆ 3 tbsp extra virgin olive oil
- ◆ Small handful of large-grated Parmesan

Boil the pasta in salted water until *al dente*. Drain, rinse with cold water and drain again. Pour the noodles into a bowl and add the courgettes, basil, lemon, oil and Parmesan. Season with salt and pepper, mix well and refrigerate until needed. (Keeps for two days.)

Variations
add cherry tomatoes, chopped salami, mozzarella balls, shredded chicken, peas or toasted pine nuts if you're allowed

Ketchup manis is sweet soy sauce, which is a perfect ready-made sauce for tossing noodles. Waitrose and Sainsbury's both stock it, as do Asian shops.

Noodles with broccoli and carrots

Makes 4 salads
- ◆ 200g/7oz ramen, rice or other Asian egg noodles
- ◆ 2 handfuls broccoli florets
- ◆ 1 handful shredded carrot
- ◆ 125ml/4fl oz ketchup manis (or substitute soy sauce mixed with 3 tbsp sugar)
- ◆ Juice of 1 lime

Boil the noodles in salted water. When they are nearly done, add the broccoli and cook both *al dente*. Drain, rinse in cold water and drain again. Tip the noodles into a bowl and add the shredded carrot. Mix the ketchup manis with the lime juice and pour over everything. Mix well and refrigerate until needed. (Will keep for two days.)

Variations

try a tablespoon of chopped fresh ginger, chopped beef or chicken, or toasted sesame seeds

Meat- or cheese-filled pasta is perfect for protein and a good base for additional vegetables.

Tortellini pasta salad

Makes 4 salads
- ◆ 250g/8oz fresh tortellini pasta
- ◆ 10 cherry tomatoes, halved
- ◆ 2 tbsp balsamic vinegar
- ◆ 4 tbsp extra virgin olive oil

Boil the pasta in salted water until it floats to the top. Gently drain, rinse with cold water and drain again. Place in a bowl with the tomatoes, vinegar and oil. Season with salt and pepper and gently mix. Refrigerate until needed. (Will keep for two days.)

Variations
use salad cream or pesto in place of the oil and vinegar. Add chopped carrots, blanched broccoli, Parmesan or chopped fresh basil

You can add any cooked meat to this, like chicken, lamb
or beef.

Orange couscous salad with apricots and feta

Makes 4 salads
- ◆ 200g/7oz couscous
- ◆ 4 ready-soaked apricots, finely chopped
- ◆ ½ tsp salt
- ◆ 125ml/4fl oz orange juice
- ◆ 200g/7oz feta cheese, cut into cubes
- ◆ 3 tbsp extra virgin olive oil

Place the couscous in a medium bowl with the apricots
and salt. Heat the orange juice in a small saucepan
until boiling. Pour over the couscous and let sit for ten
minutes until it is all absorbed. Break up the grains with
your fingers until there are no lumps. Add the feta
cheese and olive oil and mix well. Refrigerate until
needed. (Keeps for two or three days.)

Variations

*try chopped herbs like parsley or coriander. Add any
veggies or fruit*

Pulses are considered one of the most important healthy foods to eat but need some tarting up in order to taste good. Use this as a base for any meat or veg.

Lentil salad with bacon, cheese and celery

Makes 4 salads
- ◆ 200g/7oz puy or brown lentils
- ◆ 1 stalk celery, diced
- ◆ 2 tbsp balsamic or red wine vinegar
- ◆ 3 tbsp extra virgin olive oil
- ◆ 100g/3½oz bacon or pancetta, fried until crisp
- ◆ 4 tbsp cheese – grated Parmesan or Cheddar, or feta, cubed

Boil the lentils until *al dente* and drain. While they are warm, add the celery, vinegar, oil and bacon. Mix well, then add seasoning and the cheese. Refrigerate until needed. (Keeps for two days.)

Variations
fresh herbs like dill, parsley or basil. Try chicken, lamb, cherry tomatoes, green beans, sweetcorn or chopped red pepper

This is another good dressing for egg noodles.

Sesame noodles with shredded chicken

Makes 4 salads
- ◆ 250g/8oz Chinese egg noodles or short pasta like penne
- ◆ 5 tbsp balsamic vinegar
- ◆ 3 tbsp soy sauce
- ◆ 2 tbsp sesame oil
- ◆ 2 tbsp honey
- ◆ 2 tbsp sesame seeds
- ◆ A handful of shredded chicken

Boil the noodles in salted water until *al dente*. In a medium bowl, mix together the vinegar, soy, sesame oil and honey. Drain the noodles and mix while warm with the sauce. Let cool slightly and then add the sesame seeds and chicken. Keeps for two days.

Variations

if they like spicy food, add some crushed chillies. Shredded carrot, cucumber, diced red pepper would be nice as well. Or blanch some broccoli when you cook the noodles

Kids like the 'bits' in the salad more than the lettuce, so why not let them have just that?

Chopped salad

Makes 1 salad

- ◆ 3 slices salami, shredded chicken, bacon or ham, roughly chopped
- ◆ ¼ red pepper, diced
- ◆ A small chunk of cheese – Cheddar, Gruyère or Gouda, diced
- ◆ 1 small carrot, diced
- ◆ 1 small chunk iceberg lettuce, ripped into pieces
- ◆ Your favourite salad dressing

Arrange the ingredients in a container, leaving out the dressing. Pour some of the dressing into a small plastic bag and tie it in a knot. They can then use this later to dress the salad without it going soggy. Use on the day.

Variations

add other veggies like cucumber, sunflower seeds or celery. For the more daring, add beetroot or a few tinned chickpeas

If you live anywhere near a Middle Eastern shop, try to buy some cucumbers from them: they are tiny and incredibly tasty. Otherwise, buy organic – the flavour is much better than that of the hothouse ones.

Little Greek macaroni salad

Makes 4 salads
◆ 60g/2oz macaroni or other small pasta
◆ 6 tinned black olives
◆ Handful of diced cucumber
◆ Handful of cherry tomatoes, halved
◆ 200g/7oz feta cheese, cubed
◆ 2 tbsp red wine vinegar
◆ 3 tbsp extra virgin olive oil

Boil the pasta in salted water. Drain, rinse with cold water and drain again. Place in a bowl with the olives, cucumber, tomatoes, feta, vinegar and oil. Season with salt and pepper and toss together. Refrigerate until needed. (Keeps for two days.)

Variations

if you can do it . . . diced red onion or a little oregano or chopped dill. Add shredded chicken or leftover lamb

Balsamic vinegar is great to start your kids on because it's sweet and not overly tart.

Tuna, cherry tomato and potato salad

Makes 1 salad
- ◆ Half a tin tuna fish, drained (tuna steak in olive oil is nice)
- ◆ Handful of cherry tomatoes, halved
- ◆ Half a stick of celery, diced
- ◆ 4–5 tiny new potatoes, boiled and cut in half
- ◆ 1 tsp balsamic or red wine vinegar, or squeeze of lemon
- ◆ 1 tbsp olive oil

Arrange the tuna, cherry tomatoes, celery and potatoes in a container. Drizzle with the vinegar and oil and season with salt and pepper. Keeps for two days in the fridge.

Variations
use your favourite bottled dressing, add spinach leaves or use chicken in place of the tuna. Tinned cannellini beans are nice instead of potatoes

This is a great use for leftover rice. Never let rice sit too long at room temperature: refrigerate it straight away to prevent any potential health hazards. Be sure to keep the salad chilled properly in the lunch box with a frozen yogurt or juice.

Rice, chicken and sweetcorn salad

Makes 1 salad
- ◆ 2 handfuls cooked white or brown rice
- ◆ 1 handful chopped roasted chicken
- ◆ 4 tbsp drained tinned sweetcorn
- ◆ 4 cherry tomatoes, halved
- ◆ 1 tbsp red wine vinegar
- ◆ 2 tbsp extra virgin olive oil

Toss all of the ingredients together in a medium bowl. Season with salt and pepper and refrigerate until needed.

Variations
chopped fresh basil, chopped pineapple, diced red pepper or carrot. You can use your favourite bottled dressing instead of the vinegar and oil

Children seem to like either fruit or vegetables, but rarely both. One of my boys is crazy for fruit. The other won't touch it, but will gladly eat broccoli and beetroot. Pre-chopped fruit from the supermarket can be useful when buying more exotic types.

Ricotta cheese with blueberries, mango and pineapple

Makes 1 salad
- ◆ 1 good scoop of ricotta cheese
- ◆ 2 tbsp blueberries
- ◆ 1 chunk of peeled mango, cut into bite-sized pieces
- ◆ 1 chunk of fresh pineapple, cut into bite-sized pieces

Arrange everything in a container and refrigerate until needed.

Variations

use any fruit your child likes – strawberries, passion fruit, raspberries, bananas, sliced oranges or watermelon. Use yogurt, fromage frais or cottage cheese

Kids like soy dressings because of the salt . . . and bottled teriyaki sauce is easy to use.

Noodles with prawns and cucumber

Makes 4 salads
- 150g/5½oz thin oriental noodles – ramen or wheat
- 2 tbsp vegetable or sesame oil
- 5 tbsp teriyaki sauce or soy sauce
- Juice of half a lemon
- 2 handfuls small cooked prawns or shredded chicken
- 2 handfuls diced cucumber
- 2 handfuls cherry tomatoes, halved

Boil the noodles in salted water until cooked. Drain and pour into a medium bowl. Pour the oil, teriyaki (or soy) sauce and lemon juice over and toss. When cool, add the prawns, cucumber and cherry tomatoes. Refrigerate until needed.

Variations

extra veggies like shredded carrot, broccoli, baby sweetcorn, or chicken

Chicken couscous with honey mustard dressing

Makes 4 salads
- 90ml/3fl oz chicken stock, boiling
- 200g/7oz couscous
- 1 large handful shredded chicken
- Half a red pepper, cut into pieces
- 2 tbsp olive oil
- 1 tbsp red wine vinegar
- 1 tsp Dijon mustard
- 1 tsp honey

Pour the hot stock over the couscous. Let sit for ten minutes and then break up with your hands or a fork until all the grains are separated. Add the chicken and peppers. In a small jam jar mix together the oil, vinegar, mustard and honey. Season with salt and pepper and shake well with the lid on. Pour the dressing over the salad and mix. Will keep for two days in the fridge.

Variations

add leftover lamb cubes, or feta, parsley, coriander, black olives and ground cumin

This dressing would be nice on pasta as well. Add any meat, chicken, salami or ham you like. Use basil pesto on this as well.

Sun-dried tomato pesto rice

Makes 4 salads
- ◆ 4 handfuls cooked white or brown rice
- ◆ 2 tbsp extra virgin olive oil
- ◆ 2 tbsp sun-dried tomato paste
- ◆ 1 tsp red wine vinegar
- ◆ 1 carrot, peeled and diced
- ◆ 1 stick celery, diced

In a medium bowl mix all the ingredients together. Season with salt and pepper. Refrigerate until needed.

Variations
any extra veggies you want to add like cherry tomatoes, red peppers, spring onions. Add cubes of Cheddar or tiny mozzarella balls

Anything crunchy is usually popular and croutons fit the bill where that is concerned.

Tomato, crouton and mozzarella salad

Makes 1 salad
- ◆ 1 handful cherry tomatoes, halved
- ◆ 1 handful toasted bread cubes, pitta or bought croutons
- ◆ 4 mini mozzarella balls (*bocconcini*)
- ◆ Small handful basil leaves, chopped
- ◆ Your favourite salad dressing or 1 tbsp balsamic vinegar and 2 tbsp olive oil

In a medium bowl, toss all of the ingredients together. Do this just before school and the dressing will be OK for lunch-time.

Variations

add other crunchy veggies like red pepper, cucumber or celery

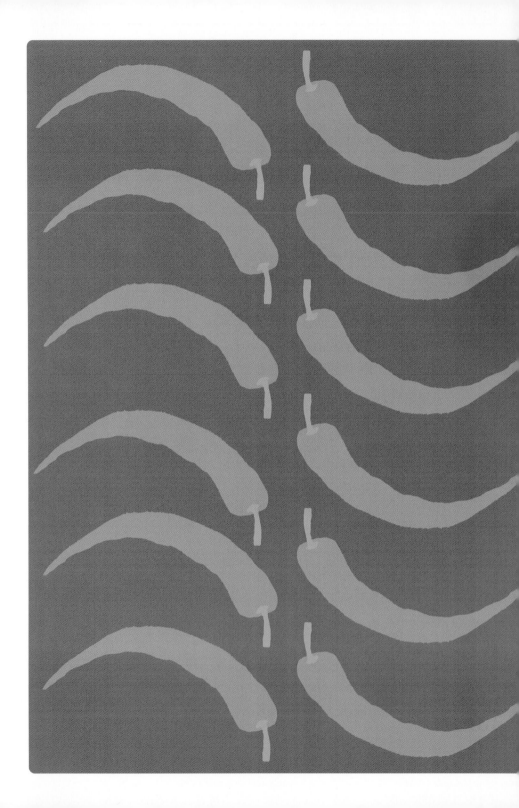

Stuff to
make ahead

Come winter, some children like to take hot food in a Thermos flask or have something more substantial to eat cold. As these take more time to make, prepare the recipes for an evening meal and save some for lunches. You may also want to think about freezing individual portions so that you can have them on hand during busy weeks. (Feel free to be smug about this with other school mums.)

Things to buy
- ◆ Cartons of soup
- ◆ Sausage rolls
- ◆ Quality chilli
- ◆ Organic baked beans (add some cooked slices of sausage)
- ◆ Samosas
- ◆ Mini quiches or tarts

Since these are wrapped and enclosed, it gives you the opportunity to add something healthy that might not get noticed amongst the tasty sausage. Choose what's in your remit.

Home-made sausage rolls

Makes 6 rolls
◆ 6 good-quality pork sausages (about 500g/1lb)
◆ 1 egg, beaten, for brushing
◆ 375g/13oz pack of ready-rolled puff pastry

Preheat the oven to 200°C, gas mark 6. Unwrap the pastry and cut into six squares. If not pre-rolled, then roll out to about a quarter of an inch thick. Brush the edges of the pastry with the egg and place a sausage on each square. Fold one side over and then press down to seal. Make two slashes across the top so that the steam can come out. Brush the top with more egg. Cook on a baking tray lined with parchment paper for twenty-five minutes. Freeze them uncooked, thaw in the fridge, and cook as above. These sausage rolls will keep for three days, refrigerated.

Variation

Add spinach or diced carrot inside

Using a muffin tin to make individual pies is extremely useful. Try other fillings like pizza ingredients. Apricots are sweet and go nicely with turkey or chicken. Add some ground cumin if you want a stronger taste.

Turkey, carrot and apricot pies

Makes 6 pies
◆ 1 tbsp olive oil
◆ 1 small onion, diced
◆ 1 large carrot, peeled and diced
◆ 750g/1lb 10oz turkey pieces
◆ 1 egg, beaten
◆ 6 ready-soaked apricots, finely chopped

Preheat the oven to 200°C, gas mark 6. Heat the olive oil in a frying pan and cook the onion and carrot for three minutes. Add the turkey and season with salt and pepper. Transfer the mixture to a bowl and add the beaten egg and the apricots. Unwrap the pastry and roll it out slightly larger than it already is – about 5mm/¼ inch thick. Cut out six squares. Push each piece of dough into a large muffin tin. Divide the filling into each and fold the excess pastry over the top. Bake for 25 minutes, then allow to cool on a rack. These will keep for two days in the fridge.

Here is another good filling for these pies.

Ham, pea and potato pies

Makes 8 pies
- ◆ 375g/13oz ready-rolled puff pastry
- ◆ 200g/7oz fresh shelled peas
- ◆ 2 handfuls chopped thick ham
- ◆ 1 large red potato, boiled, peeled and diced
- ◆ 100g/3½oz grated Gruyère, Cheddar or Taleggio cheese

Preheat oven to 200°C, gas mark 6. Unwrap the pastry, roll out about 5mm/¼ inch thick and cut into eight pieces. Press each one into a large muffin tin. Divide the peas, ham, potato and cheese between all of them. Fold the excess dough over the top and scrunch it together. Bake for twenty-five minutes or until golden. Allow to cool on a rack. Will keep for two days.

You eat cold drumsticks on picnics, so why not in a lunch box?

Honey and paprika chicken drumsticks

- 1 tbsp paprika (the Spanish sweet and smoky paprika is really good)
- 1 tsp ground cumin
- 2 tbsp honey
- Juice of half a lemon
- 1 tbsp olive oil
- 6 chicken drumsticks

In a medium bowl, mix together all the marinade ingredients. Place the chicken in the marinade and leave it for thirty minutes or overnight, refrigerated. Preheat the oven to 180°C, gas mark 4. Place the chicken pieces on a baking sheet lined with parchment paper. Season with salt and pepper and bake for forty minutes. Remove, allow to cool slightly and refrigerate until needed. Will keep for three days.

Pack these cold with a little salad cream to dip them in. You
could also throw a few sesame seeds into the coating.

Parmesan chicken pieces

◆ 100g/3½oz plain flour
◆ 3 eggs, beaten
◆ 3 handfuls of toasted fine breadcrumbs
◆ 2 handfuls of grated Parmesan
◆ 4 chicken breasts, cut into finger-sized strips
◆ Spray of olive oil

Preheat the oven to 200°C, gas mark 6. Place the flour
and eggs in separate bowls. In a third bowl, mix the
breadcrumbs, Parmesan and some salt and pepper. Line
a baking sheet with parchment paper. Season the
chicken and dip each strip in flour, then egg and finally
in the breadcrumbs. Place them on a baking tray and
spray them with a little olive oil. Bake for twenty minutes
until crisp and golden. Will keep for three days,
refrigerated.

Microwave some of this soup in the morning and pour in to
an insulated flask. To cook basmati rice, boil it with plenty
of water, drain and then rinse with cold water. Drain again
and then refrigerate it until needed.

Roasted tomato soup with rice

- ◆ 750g/1lb 10oz very ripe large plum tomatoes,
  cut in half
- ◆ 2 tbsp olive oil
- ◆ 2 tbsp unsalted butter
- ◆ 1 onion, finely chopped
- ◆ 2 sticks celery, finely diced
- ◆ 2 cloves garlic, finely chopped
- ◆ 500ml/16fl oz chicken stock
- ◆ 60g/2oz cooked basmati rice

Preheat the oven to 200°C, gas mark 6. Place the tomato
halves on a baking tray and drizzle with the olive oil.
Season with salt and pepper, and roast in the oven for
twenty minutes.

Meanwhile, heat the butter in a medium saucepan. Sauté
the onion, celery, garlic and some salt and pepper in the
butter for about ten minutes until very soft. Add the
roasted tomatoes when done, along with the stock. Cook
for five minutes and then purée in a blender or food
processor. Add the rice to the soup and serve. This will
keep for three days, refrigerated, and freezes well too.

I've never met a child who didn't like sweetcorn.

Cream of sweetcorn, potato and bacon soup

- 1 large onion, chopped
- 1 large baking potato, peeled and chopped
- 3 rashers streaky bacon, chopped into small pieces
- 4 tbsp butter
- Two 200g/7oz tins sweetcorn, drained
- 600ml/1 pint chicken stock
- 75ml/2fl oz single cream

In a large saucepan, sauté the onion, potato, bacon and butter with some salt and pepper. Cook for eight minutes, add the corn and sauté for five more minutes. Add the stock and cook for ten minutes and then add the cream. Alternatively, you can purée the soup when it is cooked, but don't add the cream until it is puréed. Will keep for two days and freezes well.

Don't be put off by the long list of ingredients: this isn't
difficult to make and contains so many healthy vegetables
and beans. Save time and chop the vegetables in a food
processor. If you have a sworn bean-hater, then purée the
soup before adding the pasta.

Pasta and bean soup

◆ 130g/4¾oz cubed
   pancetta (usually
   stocked next to salami)
◆ 1 large onion, diced
◆ 3 celery sticks, diced
◆ 2 carrots, diced
◆ 1 clove garlic, chopped
◆ 1 tbsp fresh rosemary,
   chopped

◆ 50ml/16fl oz chicken
   stock
◆ 700ml/1¼pints passata
   or tinned peeled plum
   tomatoes, puréed
◆ 400g/14oz tin borlotti
   or cannellini beans or
   chickpeas, drained
◆ 60g/2oz dried tiny pasta

In a medium saucepan, brown the pancetta for four
minutes and then remove. Add the onion, celery, carrots,
garlic, rosemary and a sprinkle of salt and pepper. Sauté
in the olive oil for ten minutes on a low heat until the
onion is translucent. Add the pancetta, stock, passata
and beans and cook on a low heat for thirty minutes.
Meanwhile, boil the pasta in salted water until cooked.
Drain and add to the soup when it is finished. This keeps
for one week, refrigerated, or freezes well.

Fresh tortellini are immensely useful for soups and salads.
Using chicken on the bone makes the stock taste more
flavourful. If you find it too fiddly taking it off the bones,
then use breasts.

Chicken and tortellini soup

- ◆ 3 tbsp olive oil
- ◆ 1 medium onion, chopped
- ◆ 3 sticks celery, sliced
- ◆ 3 carrots, peeled and sliced
- ◆ 1 clove garlic, chopped
- ◆ 2 chicken legs, skin removed
- ◆ 500ml/16fl oz chicken stock
- ◆ 250g/8oz fresh tortellini boiled in salted water until cooked

In a large saucepan, heat the olive oil. Add the onion,
celery, carrot, garlic and some salt and pepper. Sauté for
ten minutes on a low heat and then add the chicken
legs. Brown them slightly and then add the chicken
stock. Cook on a medium-to-low heat with a lid for thirty
minutes. Remove the chicken and use a fork to take the
meat off the bones. Place the meat back in the soup
along with the tortellini. This keeps for one week,
refrigerated, or freezes well.

Meatballs are irresistible to both children and adults. My Italian mother used to make this when I was a child. Baby spinach dropped in it is very good as well.

Tiny meatball and pasta soup

For the meatballs
◆ 200g/7oz pork or beef mince
◆ 1 small onion, very finely chopped
◆ 1 egg
◆ 2 tbsp breadcrumbs
◆ 2 tbsp chopped parsley
◆ 1 tbsp grated Parmesan cheese

For the soup
◆ 2 tbsp olive oil
◆ 1 small onion, chopped
◆ 1 carrot, peeled and diced
◆ 1 litre/1¾pints chicken stock
◆ 60g/2oz tiny baby pasta, like pastina, boiled in salted water until *al dente*
◆ More grated Parmesan, to serve

In a small bowl, mix together the meatball ingredients and season with salt and pepper. Using a teaspoon, roll them into tiny meatballs and set aside. In a large saucepan, heat the olive oil and add the onion, carrot and some seasoning. Sauté for five minutes and then add the chicken stock. Bring to the boil and then add the meatballs, gently dropping them in. Cook for eight to ten minutes and then add the pasta. Serve with a bit of grated Parmesan. Keeps for one week, refrigerated, or freezes well.

Pack a few corn tortilla chips with this or a little leftover rice.

Beef chilli with beans

◆ 500g/1lb beef mince or stewing beef, cut into small cubes
◆ 3 tbsp olive oil
◆ 1 medium onion, chopped
◆ 1 red pepper, diced
◆ 2 cloves garlic, chopped
◆ 2 tbsp mild chilli powder
◆ 1 tbsp ground cumin
◆ 1 tsp paprika
◆ Two 400g/14oz tins of peeled plum tomatoes, puréed
◆ 400g/14oz tin of kidney, black or borlotti beans, drained

Heat one tablespoon of oil in a large saucepan and brown the beef on all sides. Remove from pan and add the remaining oil. Add the onion, red pepper, garlic and some salt and pepper. Sauté for five minutes on a medium heat and then add the chilli powder, cumin, paprika, puréed tomatoes and beans. Cook, covered, on a medium-to-low heat, for thirty to forty minutes until tender. Will keep for one week, refrigerated. Freezes well.

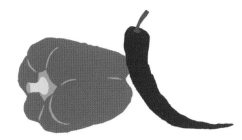

Sweets
and treats

Some of these are really good for you, others not, and the rest sort of. Once a week, put in something decadent – they should be rewarded for their efforts. At least you know what it's made of. Other days, try muffins or cookies with dried fruit. Most of these need to be prepared ahead, with the exception of the fruit ideas.

Things to buy

- Any fruit – blueberries, cherries, strawberries, kiwis, blackberries, peaches, nectarines, plums, grapes, pears, apples, oranges
- Penguin bars (the packages are so cool and it's a small treat)
- Chunk of dark chocolate
- Meringues
- Fromage frais with fruit in tubs
- Yogurt- or chocolate-covered raisins
- Amaretti biscuits
- Italian biscotti

Dulce de leche is a caramel sauce made from slowly cooked milk and sugar, with the consistency of peanut butter. Surprisingly, it's not as evil as one might think: it's calorific but extremely high in calcium. If it promotes eating an apple a day, then why not? Your family could soon be buying cases of it.

Apples and pears with caramel sauce

- ◆ 1 small apple or pear, cored and cut into quarters
- ◆ 3 tbsp *Dulce de leche* caramel sauce (sold at all major supermarkets near ice-cream toppings) or Nutella (if allowed)

Put the caramel sauce in a container with the fruit.

This makes more chocolate sauce than you will use, but you need to melt enough to be able to dip the fruit in. Chopped nuts (peanuts, cashews, pistachios) are delicious for rolling the chocolate-coated fruit in, but only if allowed.

Chocolate-dipped strawberries and bananas

◆ 60g/2oz plain chocolate
◆ 15 strawberries, cleaned, with tops on, and/or
   1 banana, cut into chunks

Melt the chocolate in a glass bowl in a microwave for one and a half minutes or place it in a large glass bowl over a small saucepan of simmering water. Line a baking tray with non-stick baking paper. Use a skewer for the bananas and dip both fruits in chocolate. Place on the tray and refrigerate for a couple of hours. These will keep for a couple of days, refrigerated.

If you have a mango lover in the family, use one mango over two days or serve the other half at breakfast.

Hedgehog mango

◆ 1 small mango

Slice the two cheeks (sides) off the mango stone. Cut each one into two pieces lengthways. Without cutting into the skin, cut a criss-cross pattern into the flesh of the fruit. Show your child how to bend the fruit inside out and they can eat it straight from the skin in bite-sized pieces. Wrap in a plastic bag.

Of course, you can easily buy this ready-made in tubs, but wouldn't it be nice to get some extra fruit in without the preservatives and sugar? Berries are one of the top fifty power foods, so it's worth doing.

Fruit fool with fromage frais

- 100g/3½oz crushed or puréed fruit – blueberries, cherries, strawberries, kiwis, blackberries, peaches, nectarines, plums, grapes, pears, apples, oranges
- 1 tbsp caster sugar
- 100g/3½oz fromage frais

Purée or crush the fruit and add the sugar. Swirl the fromage frais through and pack some in a small container with a fitted lid.

Although meringues are loaded with sugar, they don't contain hefty quantities of butter like most puddings.

Mini meringues with hundreds and thousands

Makes 16 small meringues
- 5 egg whites – room temperature
- Pinch of salt
- 300g/10oz caster sugar
- 1 tsp vinegar
- 3 tbsp hundreds and thousands or tiny silver balls

Preheat the oven to 180°C, gas mark 4. Line a baking tray with parchment paper. Place the egg whites in a very clean mixing bowl with the salt. It's important that there is no grease in the bowl, or it can affect how the egg whites whip. Using the whisk attachment on a mixer, whisk the whites until they are stiff. Slowly pour in the sugar, a spoonful at a time, until it's all added. At this point it should be glossy and very stiff. Fold in the cornflour and vinegar. Use a tablespoon to measure the mixture onto the baking sheet and sprinkle each spoonful with the decorations.

Bake in the oven for five minutes and then lower the heat to 130°C, gas mark 1, for forty-five minutes. Allow to cool to room temperature and then remove from the paper onto a cooling rack. They will keep in a sealed container for four to five days.

These are very fast to put together and have a fudge-like consistency. Remember them when the time comes for the cake sale at school.

Brownies with white chocolate chunks

Makes 16 small squares
- 125g/4oz unsalted butter
- 100g/3½oz plain dark chocolate
- 200g/7oz caster sugar
- 2 eggs
- 1 tsp vanilla extract
- 90g/3½oz plain flour
- Pinch of salt
- 150g/5oz white chocolate, roughly chopped

Preheat oven to 160°C, gas mark 3. Rub a deep 16cm x 20cm baking dish with butter and line with parchment paper. Melt the butter and chocolate in a large bowl set over a saucepan of simmering water. Stir until smooth. Remove from the heat and add the sugar, eggs and vanilla. Stir until combined and then add the flour and salt. Add the white chocolate, mix gently and pour into the prepared pan. Bake for thirty-five to forty minutes until a toothpick comes out clean when inserted in the centre. Cool completely and then cut into squares. These keep for three to four days in an airtight container.

Yogurt makes these muffins moist and light. Try other fruits like chopped peaches or whatever is in season.

Blackberry and apple muffins

Makes 12 large or 24 mini muffins
- ◆ 150g/5oz soft brown sugar
- ◆ 1 tsp vanilla
- ◆ 1 egg, lightly beaten
- ◆ 125ml/4fl oz vegetable oil or melted butter (depending on how healthy you want them to be)
- ◆ 300g/10oz self-raising flour
- ◆ 175ml/6fl oz plain yogurt
- ◆ 180g/5½oz fresh blackberries or raspberries
- ◆ 1 apple, peeled, cored and cut into small chunks

Preheat the oven to 180°C, gas mark 4. Place cupcake liners in a six-hole muffin tin. In a medium bowl, mix the sugar, vanilla, egg and oil. Mix in the flour next and then fold the yogurt through. Don't over-mix or the muffins will be heavy. Fold in the fruit and spoon the mixture into the papers. Bake for twenty-five minutes until golden. Will keep for three days in an airtight container.

These are healthier than most muffins that use butter. Pure vegetable oil has good fats (monounsaturated) versus butter, which contains saturated fat.

Blueberry and coconut muffins

Makes 6 large or 12 mini muffins
- ◆ 150g/5oz soft brown sugar
- ◆ 1 tsp vanilla
- ◆ 1 egg, lightly beaten
- ◆ 125ml/4fl oz pure vegetable oil
- ◆ 300g/10oz self-raising flour
- ◆ 175ml/6fl oz plain yogurt
- ◆ 175g/6oz fresh blueberries or other berries such as raspberries
- ◆ 4 tbsp desiccated coconut

Preheat the oven to 180°C, gas mark 4. Place cupcake liners in a six-hole muffin tin. In a medium bowl, mix the sugar, vanilla, egg and oil. Mix in the flour and coconut next and then fold the yogurt through. Don't over-mix or the muffins will be heavy. Fold in the fruit and spoon the mixture into the paper cases. Bake for twenty to twenty-five minutes until golden. Will keep for three days in an airtight container.

**My five sisters and I would make these as kids and they
were my absolute favourite. If you are not sure about making
your own caramel, then melt down some chewy toffees and
stir them into the popcorn.**

Caramel popcorn balls

- 1½ tbsp unsalted butter
- 350g/12oz brown sugar
- 6 tbsp water
- 175g/6oz popping corn
- 3 tbsp vegetable oil

In an old heavy pot with a fitted lid, heat the oil and
popcorn and, when it starts popping, place the lid on.
Cook until you don't hear any kernels popping and then
immediately pour into a large mixing bowl.

In a heavy medium saucepan, heat the butter over low
heat. Add the sugar and water, stir until mixed and bring
to a boil. Allow to boil for one minute, but don't stir, and
then remove from heat. Pour over the popcorn and stir
gently to mix. Line a baking tray with non-stick baking
paper. Tip the popcorn out onto it. When cool enough to
handle, oil your hands and make small balls. Wrap
individually in waxy or non-stick baking paper.

Frosted cupcakes can be messy in lunch boxes, so this one
has a cream cheese filling on the inside. Besides being very
tidy, they taste delicious.

Chocolate cupcakes with cream cheese filling

Makes 16 cupcakes
For the filling
◆ 250g/8oz cream cheese
◆ 60g/2oz caster sugar
◆ 1 egg

For the cupcakes
◆ 200g/7oz plain flour
◆ 200g/7oz caster sugar
◆ 30g/1oz cocoa powder
◆ 1 tsp baking soda
◆ Pinch of salt

◆ 250ml/8fl oz water
◆ 4 tbsp melted butter
◆ 75ml/2½fl oz vegetable
   oil
◆ 1 egg, beaten
◆ 1 tsp vanilla

Preheat the oven to 160°C, gas mark 3. In a small bowl,
beat the cream cheese, sugar and egg and set aside. Sift
the dry ingredients together in a large mixing bowl. Pour
the water into a measuring jug and add the butter, oil,
beaten egg and vanilla. Pour into the dry ingredients and
whisk until smooth, but don't over-mix. Place cupcake
cases in a deep muffin tin. Place a spoonful of the cream
cheese filling in each cup and then divide the batter
between all the cups, pouring it over the top. Bake for
twenty to twenty-five minutes, remove from the pan and
leave to cool on a rack.

Oats are filled with vitamins galore, but also have another interesting benefit – they keep you full for a long time due to their slow release of energy. Since children are hungry every five minutes (purely for snacks), these could be the answer to every mother's prayers.

Oatmeal cookies with chocolate and cherries

- ◆ 200g/7oz plain flour
- ◆ ½ tsp baking soda
- ◆ ½ tsp baking powder
- ◆ ½ tsp salt
- ◆ 250g/8oz unsalted butter
- ◆ 350g/12oz soft brown sugar
- ◆ 45g/1½oz caster sugar
- ◆ 2 eggs
- ◆ 2 tsp vanilla
- ◆ 75g/3oz small dried cherries, finely chopped
- ◆ 350g/12oz porridge oats
- ◆ 200g/7oz chocolate pieces or chips

Preheat the oven to 180°C, gas mark 4. Mix the flour, baking soda, baking powder and salt in a medium mixing bowl and set aside. Using a free-standing or hand-held mixer, or a wooden spoon, cream together the butter, sugars, eggs and vanilla. Stir in the flour mixture and then add the cherries, oats and chocolate pieces. Line two baking sheets with non-stick baking paper. Drop tablespoonfuls of the dough onto the sheets and press down gently. Bake for eight to ten minutes until golden. Remove from the sheets and leave to cool on a rack. These will keep for one week in an airtight container.

These are super-easy to make and have filling oats in them
as well.

Flapjacks with dried apricots and coconut

- ◆ 125g/4oz butter
- ◆ 3 tbsp golden syrup
- ◆ 90g/3oz demerara sugar
- ◆ 8 ready-soaked dried apricots, finely chopped
- ◆ ½ tsp cinnamon
- ◆ 150g/5oz porridge oats
- ◆ 60g/2oz desiccated coconut

Preheat oven to 160°C, gas mark 3. Grease a baking tin
approximately 22 x 16cm in size. Melt the butter, syrup
and sugar in a medium pan. Add the apricots and
cinnamon and pour in the oats and coconut. Mix together
and then pour into the tin. Bake for thirty to thirty-five
minutes. Allow to cool for five minutes, and cut into
slices while it is warm. These will keep for one week in
an airtight container.

When I was young, my mum made a salad called ambrosia with tinned fruit cocktail, marshmallows and coconut. This is a much healthier version, but you could add a few marshmallows if you want the fruit intake to go up.

Fruit salad with coconut and yogurt

Makes 1–2 salads
- Handful of strawberries, cut in half
- Handful of blueberries
- 1 kiwi, peeled and cut into small pieces
- Half a mango, peeled and cut into small pieces
- 2 tbsp sweet desiccated coconut
- 3 tbsp plain yogurt

Toss all of the ingredients together in a bowl and refrigerate until needed.

Variations

use any of your favourite fruits like bananas, pineapple, apples, grapes, oranges or peaches

Index

Apples 11
  Apples and pears with caramel sauce 109
  Blackberry and apple muffins 115
  Turkey, cheese and apple bagel 38
Apricots 11
  Apricot and cream cheese celery sticks 66
  Flapjacks with dried apricots and coconut 120
  Orange couscous salad with apricots and feta 80
  Turkey, carrot and apricot pies 96
Asparagus 12
  Asparagus and ham roll-ups 60
Avocados 11
  Avocado, bacon and cream cheese baguette 22
  Avocado, mozzarella, tomato and bacon 75
  Quick guacamole with crudités 65

Bacon
  Avocado, bacon and cream cheese baguette 22
  Avocado, mozzarella, tomato and bacon 75
  Bacon, lettuce and tomato sandwich 40
  Chopped salad 83
  Cream of sweetcorn, potato and bacon soup 101
  Lentil salad with bacon, cheese and celery 81
Bananas 10
  Chocolate-dipped strawberries and bananas 110
Beans
  Beef chilli with beans 105
  Pasta and bean soup 102
  Salami, bean and Parmesan pitta 31
  Tangy red bean dip 64
  White bean, honey and rosemary dip with breadsticks 61
Beef
  Beef and tomato sandwich 26
  Beef chilli with beans 105
Beetroot 12
  Beetroot dip with Parmesan 63
Biscuits
  Cheddar penny biscuits 69
  Oatmeal cookies with chocolate and cherries 119

Blackberries 10
  Blackberry and apple muffins 115
Blueberries 10
  Blueberry and coconut muffins 116
  Ricotta cheese with blueberries, mango and pineapple 87
Bread 15
Broccoli 12
  Broccoli pesto pasta with tomatoes 73
  Noodles with broccoli and carrots 78

Cabbage 12
Cannellini beans see Beans
Carrots 11
  Noodles with broccoli and carrots 78
  Turkey, carrot and apricot pies 96
Celery 12
  Apricot and cream cheese celery sticks 66
  Pasta with tuna, mayonnaise and celery 74
  Pitta with prawn and celery salad 41
Cheddar see Cheese
Cheese
  Avocado, mozzarella, tomato and bacon 75
  Beetroot dip with Parmesan 63
  Cheddar penny biscuits 69
  Chopped salad 83
  Cottage cheese with ham and pineapple 76
  Cream cheese with sugarsnap peas 59
  Feta, tomato and cucumber baguette 36
  Grilled halloumi, tomato and cucumber baguette 43
  Ham and cheese sandwich 24
  Ham, tomato and fresh mozzarella roll 29
  Lentil salad with bacon, cheese and celery 81
  Little Greek macaroni salad 84
  Orange couscous salad with apricots and feta 80
  Parmesan popcorn 58
  Ricotta cheese with blueberries, mango and pineapple 87
  Salami, bean and Parmesan pitta 31
  Seeded roll with Cheddar, pear and chutney 46
  Smoked trout, cheese and crackers 30
  Submarine sandwich 53
  The deli bag – ham, cheese and

crackers 37
  Tomato, crouton and mozzarella salad 91
  Turkey, cheese and apple bagel 38
Cherries 11
Cherry tomatoes see Tomatoes
Chicken
  Chicken and tortellini soup 103
  Chicken couscous with honey mustard dressing 89
  Chicken salad wrap 47
  Chicken satay baguette 45
  Chicken taco wrap 21
  Chopped salad 83
  Coronation chicken salad pitta 52
  Honey and paprika chicken drumsticks 98
  Parmesan chicken pieces 99
  Rice, chicken and sweetcorn salad 86
  Roast chicken baguette with sweet chilli dipping sauce 51
  Sesame noodles with shredded chicken 82
  Tandoori chicken pitta 33
Chickpeas
  Hummus 57
Chilli
  Beef chilli with beans 105
Chilli sauce
  Roast chicken baguette with sweet chilli dipping sauce 51
Chocolate
  Brownies with white chocolate chunks 114
  Chocolate cupcakes with cream cheese filling 118
  Chocolate-dipped strawberries and bananas 110
  Oatmeal cookies with chocolate and cherries 119
Chorizo
  Chorizo sandwiches 27
Cornichons see Pickles
Cottage cheese
  Cottage cheese with ham and pineapple 76
Courgette 12
  Pasta wheels with courgette, lemon and basil 77
Couscous
  Chicken couscous with honey mustard dressing 89

Orange couscous salad with apricots and feta 80
Crackers
 Smoked trout, cheese and crackers 30
 The deli bag – ham, cheese and crackers 37
Cream cheese
 Apricot and cream cheese celery sticks 66
 Chocolate cupcakes with cream cheese filling 118
 Cream cheese with sugarsnap peas 59
Cucumber 13
 Feta, tomato and cucumber baguette 36
 Grilled halloumi, tomato and cucumber baguette 43
 Little Greek macaroni salad 84
 Noodles with prawns and cucumber 88
 Tzatziki dip with cucumbers 62
Curry
 Coronation chicken salad pitta 52

Egg
 Egg salad sandwich 35
 Tuna, egg and lettuce wrap 28

Feta see Cheese
Flapjacks with dried apricots and coconut 120
Fromage frais
 Fruit fool with fromage frais 112
Fruit fool with fromage frais 112
Fruit salad with coconut and yogurt 121

Grapes 11
Green beans 12

Halloumi see Cheese
Ham
 Asparagus and ham roll-ups 60
 Chopped salad 83
 Cottage cheese with ham and pineapple 76
 Ham and cheese sandwich 24
 Ham, pea and potato pies 97
 Ham, tomato and fresh mozzarella roll 29
 The deli bag – ham, cheese and crackers 37
Hummus 57
 Hummus pitta with veggies 32

Jam
 Peanut butter and jam sandwich 44

Kiwi 11

Lamb
 Lamb kebab wrap 34
Lentils
 Lentil salad with bacon, cheese and celery 81
Lettuce
 Bacon, lettuce and tomato sandwich 40

Mango 10
 Hedgehog mango 111
 Ricotta cheese with blueberries, mango and pineapple 87
Marmite
 Marmite on toast 49
Meatballs
 Cold meatball pitta 39
 Tiny meatball and pasta soup 104
Meringues
 Mini meringues with hundreds and thousands 113
Mozzarella see Cheese

Noodles
 Noodles with broccoli and carrots 78
 Noodles with prawns and cucumber 88
 Sesame noodles with shredded chicken 82
Nuts
 Soy and sesame nuts 68

Olives
 Little Greek macaroni salad 84
Oranges 11

Parmesan see Cheese
Pasta
 Broccoli pesto pasta with tomatoes 73
 Chicken and tortellini soup 103
 Little Greek macaroni salad 84
 Pasta and bean soup 102
 Pasta wheels with courgette, lemon and basil 77
 Pasta with tuna, mayonnaise and celery 74
 Tiny meatball and pasta soup 104

Tortellini pasta salad 79
Peaches 11
Peanut butter
 Peanut butter and jam sandwich 44
Peas 12
 Cream cheese with sugarsnap peas 59
 Ham, pea and potato pies 97
Pears 11
 Apples and pears with caramel sauce 109
 Seeded roll with Cheddar, pear and chutney 46
Pecans see Nuts
Pesto
 Broccoli pesto pasta with tomatoes 73
 Sun-dried tomato pesto rice 90
Pickles
 French salami and pickle baguette 50
Pineapples 11
 Cottage cheese with ham and pineapple 76
 Ricotta cheese with blueberries, mango and pineapple 87
Plums 11
Popcorn
 Caramel popcorn balls 117
 Parmesan popcorn 58
Potatoes
 Cream of sweetcorn, potato and bacon soup 101
 Ham, pea and potato pies 97
 Tuna, cherry tomato and potato salad 85
Prawns
 Noodles with prawns and cucumber 88
 Pitta with prawn and celery salad 41

Raspberries 10
Rice
 Rice, chicken and sweetcorn salad 86
 Roasted tomato soup with rice 100
 Sun-dried tomato pesto rice 90
Ricotta see Cheese
Rocket 13

Salads
 Avocado, mozzarella, tomato and bacon 75
 Broccoli pesto pasta with tomatoes 73
 Chicken couscous with honey mustard dressing 89

Chopped salad 83
Cottage cheese with ham and pineapple 76
Lentil salad with bacon, cheese and celery 81
Little Greek macaroni salad 84
Noodles with broccoli and carrots 78
Noodles with prawns and cucumber 88
Orange couscous salad with apricots and feta 80
Pasta wheels with courgette, lemon and basil 77
Pasta with tuna, mayonnaise and celery 74
Rice, chicken and sweetcorn salad 86
Ricotta cheese with blueberries, mango and pineapple 87
Sesame noodles with shredded chicken 82
Sun-dried tomato pesto rice 90
Tomato, crouton and mozzarella salad 91
Tortellini pasta salad 79
Tuna, cherry tomato and potato salad 85
Salami
    Chopped salad 83
    French salami and pickle baguette 50
    Salami, bean and Parmesan pitta 31
    Submarine sandwich 53
Salt 13
Sausages
    Cold sausage sandwich 25

Home-made sausage rolls 95
Smoked salmon
    Smoked salmon, tomato and cream cheese bagels 23
Smoked trout
    Smoked trout, cheese and crackers 30
Soup
    Chicken and tortellini soup 103
    Cream of sweetcorn, potato and bacon soup 101
    Pasta and bean soup 102
    Roasted tomato soup with rice 100
    Tiny meatball and pasta soup 104
Spinach 12
    Tuna, sweetcorn and spinach roll 48
Strawberries 10
    Chocolate-dipped strawberries and bananas 110
Sugar 13
Sun-dried tomatoes
    Sun-dried tomato pesto rice 90
Sunflower seeds
    Toasted sunflower seeds 67
Sweet peppers 12
Sweetcorn 12
    Cream of sweetcorn, potato and bacon soup 101
    Rice, chicken and sweetcorn salad 86
    Tuna, sweetcorn and spinach roll 48
Tomatoes 12
    Avocado, mozzarella, tomato and

bacon 75
    Bacon, lettuce and tomato sandwich 40
    Broccoli pesto pasta with tomatoes 73
    Feta, tomato and cucumber baguette 36
    Grilled halloumi, tomato and cucumber baguette 43
    Little Greek macaroni salad 84
    Roasted tomato soup with rice 100
    Tomato, crouton and mozzarella salad 91
    Tomato, watercress and salad cream sandwich 42
    Tuna, cherry tomato and potato salad 85
Tuna
    Pasta with tuna, mayonnaise and celery 74
    Tuna, cherry tomato and potato salad 85
    Tuna, egg and lettuce wrap 28
    Tuna, sweetcorn and spinach roll 48
Turkey
    Turkey, carrot and apricot pies 96
    Turkey, cheese and apple bagel 38
Walnuts see Nuts
Watercress 12
    Tomato, watercress and salad cream sandwich 42
Watermelons 11
Yogurt
    Tzatziki dip with cucumbers 62

Acknowledgements

Huge thanks to my husband, Patrick, who patiently watched the children on Saturdays so I could work and has been so supportive of my career.

Camilla Stoddart – thank you so much for commissioning this book and having such a lovely sense of humour. I was thrilled to write this.

Lulu Grimes – for your support, friendship, and much appreciated recommendation.

Lindsey Elder – many thanks for all your invaluable nutrition and health tips.

To all my fantastic friends and the mothers in Saint Margarets who agreed to help me test recipes and make their children willing guinea pigs: Carol Tupper, Robyn Ferraz, Emma Leech, Karen Noakes, Aiofe Leopold and Shirley Jackson.

To Joss and Kaja Redler for eating so many experiments and being such outstanding judges of taste.

A big thank you to Chantal Gibbs for managing the editing process and Fiona Brown for editing my text so beautifully.

Notes

Notes

Notes